1 Look at the shape below. All measurements are in centimetres.

(a) Show that its area is given by $4x^2 + 12x$

(b) Find the value of x when the area is 40 cm^2

Answer $x =$ _____

2 (a) Find the equation of the straight line L which passes through the points (3, −4) and (1, −8).
  (**Hint: You have to learn the coordinate geometry formulae. The formulae are not given in the exam**)

Answer _____

(b) Find the equation of the straight line which passes through (−2, 5) parallel to L.

Answer _____

3 The table below shows the heights of 240 objects to the nearest centimetre.

Height *(h* cm)	1–4	5–8	9–12	13–16	17–20	21–24	25–28
Frequency	10	32	44	78	40	28	8

(a) Complete the cumulative frequency table below.

Height (less than) cm	0.5	4.5	8.5	12.5	16.5	20.5	24.5	28.5
Cumulative Frequency	0	10	42					240

(b) Draw the cumulative frequency curve on the grid below.

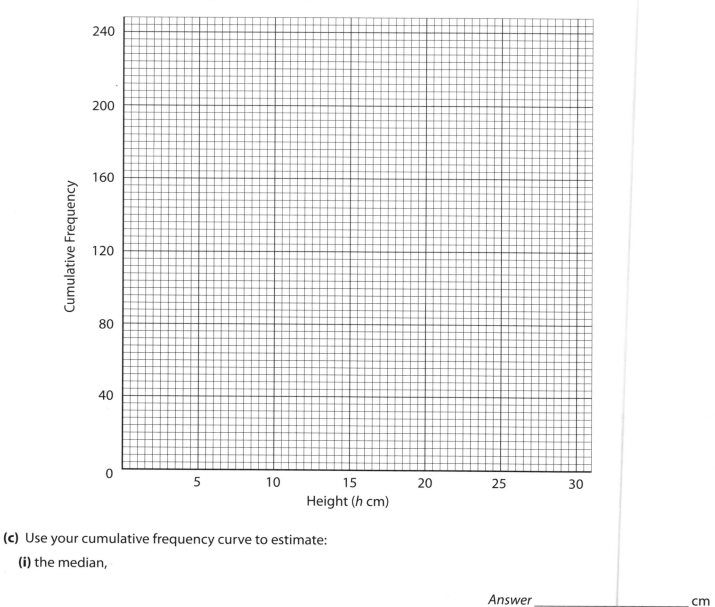

(c) Use your cumulative frequency curve to estimate:

(i) the median,

Answer _____ cm

(ii) the inter-quartile range,

Answer _____ cm

(iii) how many heights are between 7 cm and 22 cm.

Answer _____

(d) The tallest 15% are discarded. Find the tallest height kept.

Answer _____ cm

(e) Draw a box plot of the heights on the grid below.

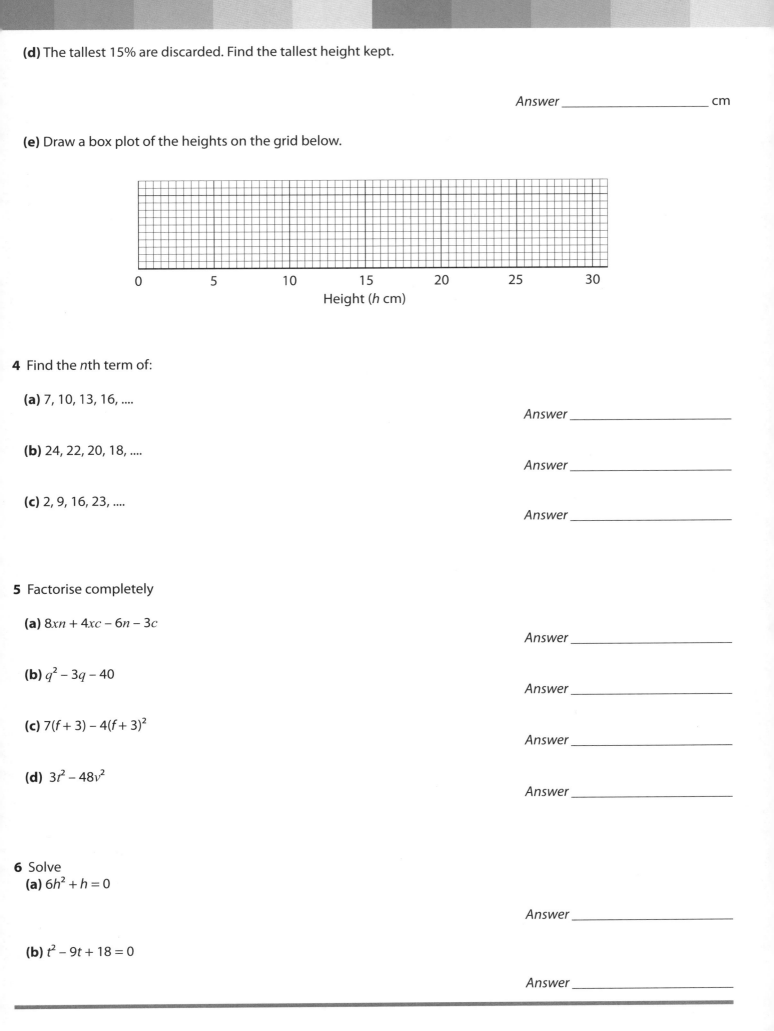

Height (*h* cm)

4 Find the *n*th term of:

(a) 7, 10, 13, 16, ...

Answer _____

(b) 24, 22, 20, 18, ...

Answer _____

(c) 2, 9, 16, 23, ...

Answer _____

5 Factorise completely

(a) $8xn + 4xc - 6n - 3c$

Answer _____

(b) $q^2 - 3q - 40$

Answer _____

(c) $7(f + 3) - 4(f + 3)^2$

Answer _____

(d) $3t^2 - 48v^2$

Answer _____

6 Solve
(a) $6h^2 + h = 0$

Answer _____

(b) $t^2 - 9t + 18 = 0$

Answer _____

7 ABC is a triangle. A(2, −4), B(3, 2), C(−3, 3). Prove that ABC is a right-angled triangle.

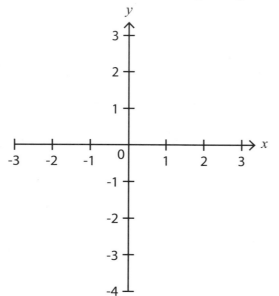

8 Show how you would calculate the following WITHOUT using a calculator:

(a) $2\frac{7}{9} \times 3\frac{2}{5}$

Answer _____

(b) $4\frac{1}{5} \div 4\frac{2}{3}$

Answer _____

(c) $5\frac{2}{3} + 2\frac{3}{4} \times 2\frac{2}{5}$

Answer _____

9 Solve the following pair of simultaneous equations.

$3x - 2y = -18$ and $2x - 7y = -46$

(Hint: You must solve these by algebra. You cannot use trial and improvement)

Answer x = _____

Answer y = _____

10 C is the centre of the circle. PQ is parallel to SR. $\angle$ PQS = 34°

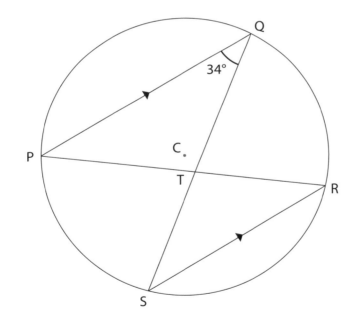

Find the size of the angle
  (a) PRS

Answer _____ °

  (b) QSR

Answer _____ °

  (c) PTQ

Answer _____ °

  (d) PCS

Answer _____ °

11 There are 976 pupils in a school.
A stratified sample by age is taken. Some information is given in the table below.

Age (years)	4 to 6	7 to 8	9	10 to 11
Number of pupils	272		144	
Number in sample	34	27		

Complete the table.

12 Solve the following:

(a) $\dfrac{9-3x}{4} = 5 - 2x$

Answer x = _____

(b) $\dfrac{2}{3}(x+1) + \dfrac{1}{4}(x-4) = 7$

Answer x = _____

(c) $\dfrac{2x-1}{3} - \dfrac{x+3}{4} = 1$

Answer x = _____

13 Simplify

(a) $\frac{m}{n} - \frac{n}{m}$

Answer _____

(b) $\frac{n}{4} + \frac{6}{n}$

Answer _____

(c) $3q - \frac{q}{4}$

Answer _____

14 The graph of $v = pm + q$ is shown below.

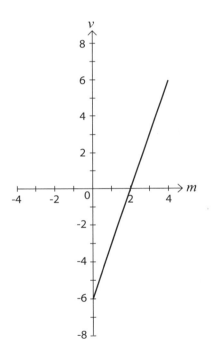

Find the value of:

(a) p

Answer $p =$ _____

(b) q

Answer $q =$ _____

15 VABCD is a rectangular based pyramid with the vertex V directly over the centre, O, of the base ABCD as shown.

AB = 6 cm BC = 8 cm VO = 6 cm

Find the size of angle VBO.

Answer _____ °

16 Two questions and possible answers from a questionaire on homework are written below.
Write down what you feel is incorrect about each of the questions and answers.
(Quality of written communication will be assessed in this question)

Question 1   How many homeworks did you have last night?

Possible Answers   1 ☐   2 ☐   3 ☐   more than 3 ☐

Answer _____

_____

Question 2   How long, T minutes, did you spend on your homework last night?

Possible Answers   T<30 ☐   30≤T<60 ☐   60≤T<120 ☐   T>120 ☐

Answer _____

_____

17 Look at the shape below. All measurements are in centimetres.

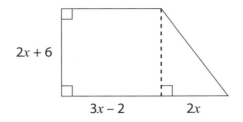

$2x + 6$

$3x - 2$ $2x$

(a) Show that its area is given by $8x^2 + 20x - 12$

(b) Find the value of x when the area is 60 cm².

Answer $x =$ _____ cm

18 (a) Find the equation of the straight line L which passes through the points $(-1, 6)$ and $(2, -6)$.
   (Hint: You have to learn the co-ordinate geometry formulae. They are not given in the formula booklet)

Answer _____

(b) Find the equation of the straight line which passes through $(3, -4)$ parallel to L.

Answer _____

(c) Find the equation of the straight line which passes through $(8, -2)$ perpendicular to L.

Answer _____

19 Solve

(a) $c^2 + 7c + 10 = 0$

Answer $c =$ _____

(b) $16f^2 = 49$

Answer $f =$ _____

(c) $w^2 + 3w - 40 = 0$

Answer $w =$ _____

20 C is the centre of the circle. TA is a tangent. $\angle ADB = 28°$

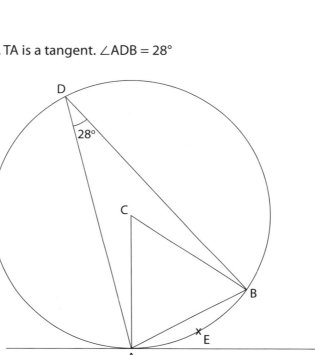

Find the sizes of the angles:
(a) ACB

Answer _____ °

(b) CAB

Answer _____ °

(c) TAB

Answer _____ °

(d) AEB

Answer _____ °

21 Solve
   (Hint: You can factorise these expressions)

   (a) $8c^2 - 50 = 0$

   Answer $c =$ _____

   (b) $2d^2 - 4d - 70 = 0$

   Answer $d =$ _____

   (c) $3e^2 - 2e - 8 = 0$

   Answer $e =$ _____

   (d) $6f^2 + 19f + 10 = 0$

   Answer $f =$ _____

   (e) $5g^2 - 30g + 40 = 0$

   Answer $g =$ _____

22 (a) What is meant by a random sample?

   Answer _____

   _____

   (b) Explain why each of the following would not be random samples.
      (i) Choosing 5 boys from each class in a primary school to represent the school.

   Answer _____

   _____

      (ii) Choosing 500 homeowners to represent the opinions of people in a town.

   Answer _____

   _____

23 A headmaster wants to take a sample of 100 pupils from the 800 pupils in his school.

(a) Suggest one way he could try to avoid bias in this sample.

Answer _____

_____

(b) Describe how he could take a stratified sample.

Answer _____

_____

24 The lengths of different objects are given below correct to the nearest centimetre.

Length (*l* cm)	1–5	6–15	16–17	18–22	23–37	38–39
Frequency	190	270	68	110	210	52

Draw a histogram on the grid below to illustrate this data.
(Hint: You must show all your working)

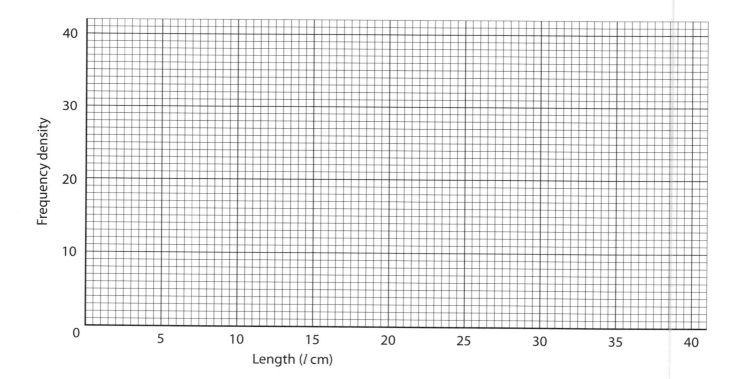

25 Prove that the opposite angles in a cyclic quadrilateral are supplementary.

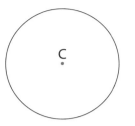

26 Expand and simplify

(a) $(4x + 3y)(2x - 7y)$

Answer _____

(b) $(5a - 6b)^2$

Answer _____

(c) $(3k - 2m)(k + 4m) - (2k + 3m)^2$

Answer _____

27 (a) Write down the equation of this straight line.

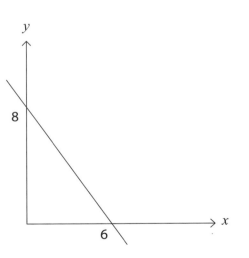

Answer _____

(b) Write down the gradient of the straight line perpendicular to the straight line drawn.

Answer _____

28 (a) The straight line $y = 3x - 4$ cuts the curve $y = x^2 - 2x - 4$ at two points.
Show that $x^2 - 5x = 0$

Answer _____

(b) Hence find the coordinates of the points where the line and curve cross.

Answer (_____,_____)

29 Solve the equation: *(Quality of written communication will be assessed in this question)*

$$\frac{2 - x}{2} - \frac{4x - 3}{3} = 13$$

Answer $x =$ _____

30 Solve

(a) $\dfrac{12}{x} + \dfrac{6}{x - 3} = 4$

Answer $x =$ _____

(b) $\dfrac{8}{x} - \dfrac{3}{x + 1} = 3$

Answer $x =$ _____

31 O is the centre of the circle. AE is a tangent and ∠EAB = 35°. ∠ABC = 52°

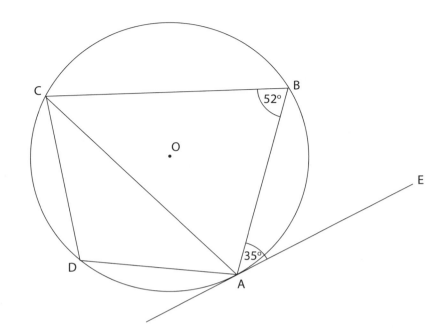

(a) Explain why ∠ACB = 35°

Answer _____

_____

(b) Explain why ∠CDA = 128°

Answer _____

_____

(c) Explain why ∠OAE = 90°

Answer _____

_____

(d) Work out the size of ∠COA

Answer _____

32 The Histogram represents the lengths, in centimetres, of objects in a box.

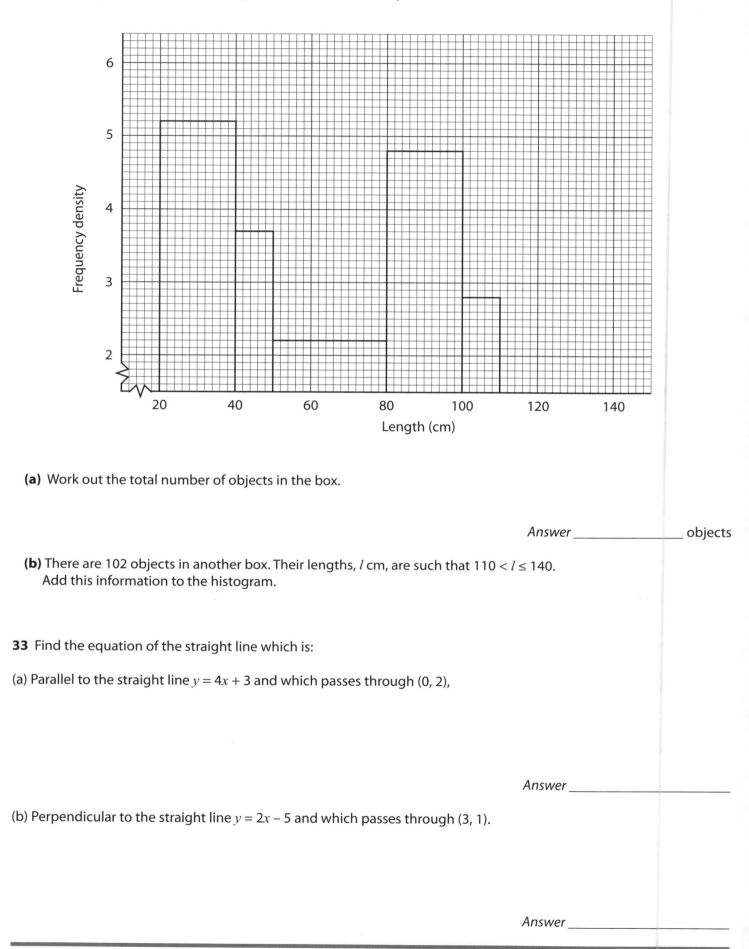

(a) Work out the total number of objects in the box.

Answer _____ objects

(b) There are 102 objects in another box. Their lengths, l cm, are such that $110 < l \leq 140$.
Add this information to the histogram.

33 Find the equation of the straight line which is:

(a) Parallel to the straight line $y = 4x + 3$ and which passes through (0, 2),

Answer _____

(b) Perpendicular to the straight line $y = 2x - 5$ and which passes through (3, 1).

Answer _____

34 Work out the following using your calculator.

(a) $7.56 \div (9.1 - 1.64)$

Answer _____

(b) $\sqrt{(5.4^3 - 2.78^2)}$

Answer _____

(c) $(4.59 \times 0.76) \div (5.84 + 1.63)$

Answer _____

(d) 2.56^7

Answer _____

35 y varies directly as the square of x. Explain what happens to y when:

(a) x is trebled

Answer _____

(b) x is halved

Answer _____

36 Find the coordinates of the two points where the straight line with equation $y = 3x - 2$ cuts the circle with equation $x^2 + y^2 = 20$

Answer (_____,_____) , (_____,_____)

37 Solve the equation:

$$\frac{5}{2x - 1} - \frac{4}{2 - x} = 5$$

Answer $x =$ _____

38 (a) p and q are integers.

$$4^p = \frac{1}{8^q}$$

Write p in terms of q.

Answer $p =$ _____

(b) Solve

$$9^{2x} = \frac{1}{3}$$

Answer $x =$ _____

39 (a) Find ∠ BAC below.
   (Hint: Give your answer correct to 1 decimal place. Make sure your calculator is in degree mode)

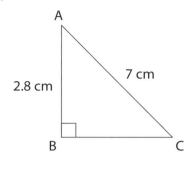

Answer _____ °

(b) Find EF.

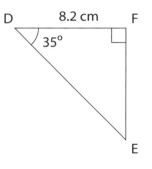

Answer _____ cm

40 A pen is measured as 14.7 cm long, correct to 1 decimal place.
   Find the least and greatest total length 7 of these pens.

Least _____ cm

Greatest _____ cm

41 Brenda deposits £P in an ISA account which pays x% compound interest each year.
After 1 year the total value of her deposit is £5824. After 2 years the total value of her deposit is £6056.96
Find **(a)** the value of x

Answer x = _____

(b) the value of P

Answer P = _____

(c) the total value of her deposit after 3 years

Answer £ _____

42 PQRS is a trapezium   PS = 9.4 cm   SR = 5.8 cm   ∠ PSR = 130°
Calculate **(a)** QR **(b)** PQ.
(Hint: Draw out a right-angled triangle)

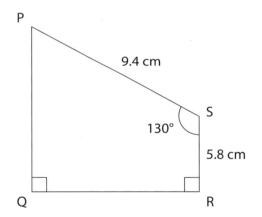

Answer (a) _____ cm

Answer (b) _____ cm

43 TP is a vertical pole. AP = 1.26 m   AB = 1.8 m
The angle of elevation of T from A is 28°.

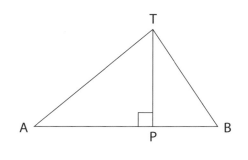

Calculate
(a) TP

Answer _____ m

(b) the angle of elevation of T from B.

Answer _____ °

44 A car depreciates by 18% per year. It originally cost £9600. After how many years will its value have halved?

Answer _____ years

45 The base radius and height of a cylindrical container were measured as 3.24 cm and 6.93 cm, each correct to the nearest one hundredth of a centimetre.

(a) 30 of these containers are stacked each on top of each other.
Calculate the maximum possible height.

Answer _____ cm

(b) 12 of these containers are placed side by side in a box.
Calculate the minimum possible width of the box.

Answer _____ cm

46 XYZ is a triangle in which XY = 6 cm, YZ = 7.2 cm and the angle XYZ = 58°.
Calculate the area of XYZ.
    (Hint: Draw a sketch. The formula for the area of a triangle is on the formula sheet)

Answer _____ cm²

47 From a point X on top of a cliff XY the angle of depression of a boat at Z is 32° as shown below. YZ = 24 m.

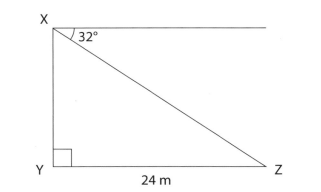

Calculate
(a) XY

Answer _____ m

(b) XZ

Answer _____ m

48 The base area and height of a cuboid were measured as 56 cm² to the nearest cm², and 8.7 cm to the nearest one tenth of a centimetre.

(a) Calculate the maximum possible volume of the cuboid.

Answer _____ cm³

The length of this cuboid was measured as 12 cm correct to the nearest centimetre.

(b) Calculate the minimum possible breadth of the cuboid.

Answer _____ cm

49 The table below gives values of v and T.

v	1	1.41	1.73	2	2.24	2.45
T	7.6	8.2	8.8	9.4	10	10.6

(a) Complete the following table giving values to the nearest integer where appropriate.

v^2	1	2				
T	7.6	8.2	8.8	9.4	10	10.6

(b) By drawing a graph on the grid below show that the relationship between v and T can be expressed as $T = av^2 + b$
(**Hint: You must explain why the equation has this form**)

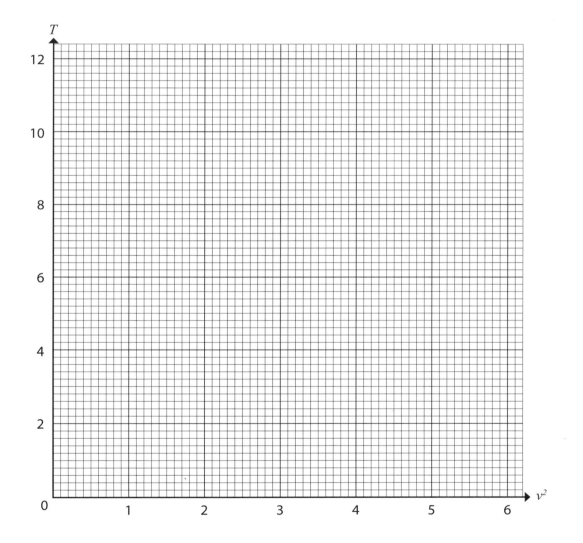

(c) Hence determine the values of **(i)** a **(ii)** b.

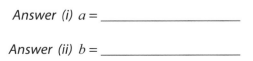

Answer (i) a = _____

Answer (ii) b = _____

50 In the diagram below BC = 9.6 cm. ∠ ADB = 42°, ∠ CBD = 54°. Calculate AB.
(**Hint: Start with the triangle in which you know 2 quantities as well as the right angle**)

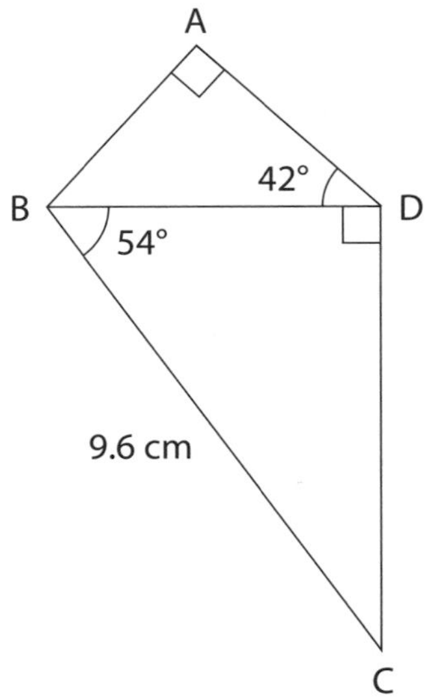

Answer _____ cm

51 Solve the following equations giving your answers to 3 decimal places.
(**Hint: The equations must not factorise as you are told to round your answers. You must then use the formula from the formula booklet**)
(**a**) $4x^2 - 7x - 8 = 0$

Answer $x =$ _____

(**b**) $6x(x + 4) = 5$

Answer $x =$ _____

52 Calculate the value of x in each diagram.
    (Hint: The formulae are in the formula booklet)

(a)

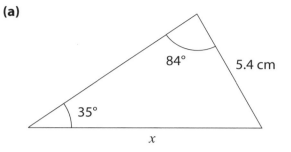

Answer $x =$ _____ cm

(b)

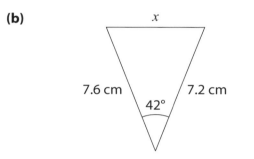

Answer $x =$ _____ cm

(c)

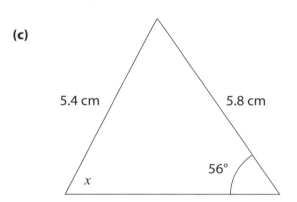

Answer $x =$ _____ °

(d)

Answer $x =$ _____ °

53 (a) Show that the equation $\dfrac{18}{x} + \dfrac{15}{x-3} = 8$ can be rearranged into the form $8x^2 - 57x + 54 = 0$

(Hint: You must show all your work. Start with the original equation and try to end up with the second equation)

(b) Hence solve $\dfrac{18}{x} + \dfrac{15}{x-3} = 8$

(Hint: Solve the quadratic equation to find x)

Answer $x =$ _____

54 XYZ is a triangle in which XY = 4.6 cm, YZ = 6.4 cm and the angle YXZ = 70°.
Calculate the area of XYZ.
(Hint: Draw a sketch.)

Answer _____ cm²

55 PQR is a triangle in which PQ = 7.4 cm, QR = 9 cm and the angle PQR = 40°.
Calculate the area of PQR.
(Hint: Draw a sketch. The formula for the area of a triangle is on the formula sheet)

Answer _____ cm²

56 ABCDEFGH is a cuboid with AB = 9 cm, BC = 6 cm and CG = 4 cm as shown below.

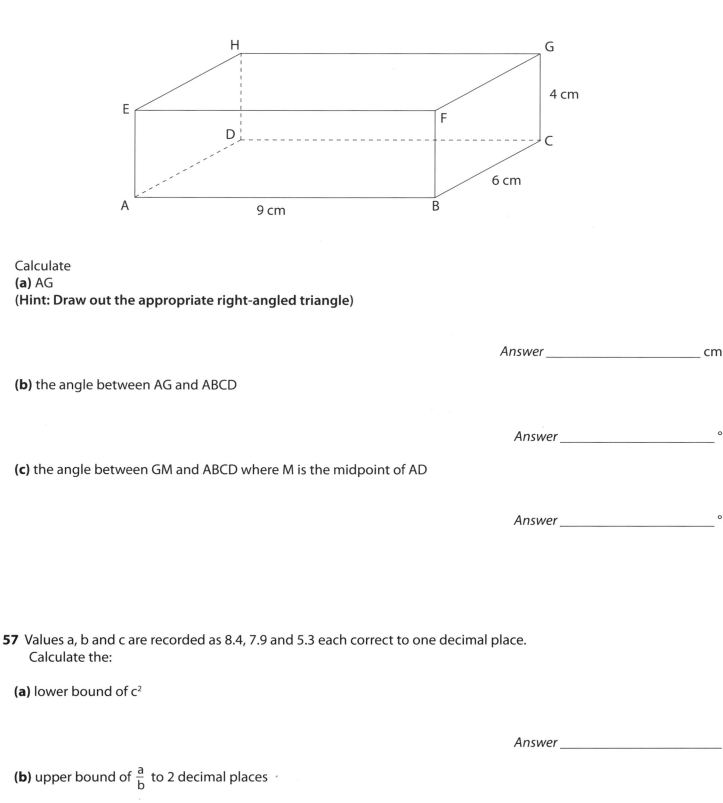

Calculate
(a) AG
(Hint: Draw out the appropriate right-angled triangle)

Answer _____ cm

(b) the angle between AG and ABCD

Answer _____ °

(c) the angle between GM and ABCD where M is the midpoint of AD

Answer _____ °

57 Values a, b and c are recorded as 8.4, 7.9 and 5.3 each correct to one decimal place.
Calculate the:

(a) lower bound of c^2

Answer _____

(b) upper bound of $\frac{a}{b}$ to 2 decimal places

Answer _____

(c) lower bound of b − c

Answer _____

58 VABCD is a rectangular based pyramid as shown below.

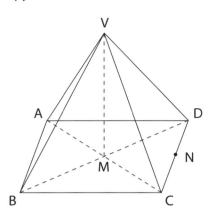

V is vertically above M, the point where the diagonals of the rectangle cross. N is the midpoint of CD. VM = 10 cm
BC = 8.5 cm.

(a) Calculate the angle between VN and ABCD.
    (Hint: Draw out the appropriate right-angled triangle)

Answer _____ °

∠ VBM = 65°
(b) Calculate the length of BD.

Answer _____ cm

(c) Calculate the length of CD.

Answer _____ cm

59 PQRS is a quadrilateral as shown below.

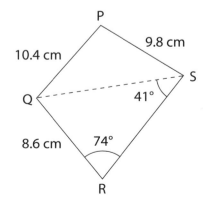

QR = 8.6 cm   QP = 10.4 cm   SP = 9.8 cm   ∠ QRS = 74° ∠ QSR = 41°
    Calculate the size of angle QPS.

Answer _____ °

60 The equation of a straight line is $y = ax + b$.
The line goes through the points (2, 13) and (−1, −11).
Work out the values of a and b.

Answer $a = $ _____

Answer $b = $ _____

61 C is the centre of the circle. TA and TB are tangents drawn from T. $\angle$ TAB = 58°.

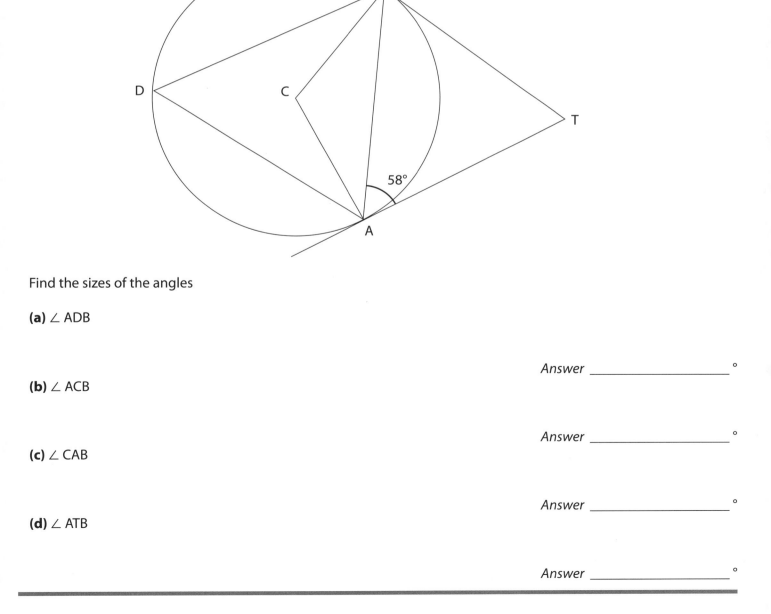

Find the sizes of the angles

(a) $\angle$ ADB

Answer _____ °

(b) $\angle$ ACB

Answer _____ °

(c) $\angle$ CAB

Answer _____ °

(d) $\angle$ ATB

Answer _____ °

62 y varies as the square of x

(a) $y = 3.2$ when $x = 2.5$
Write down a formula for y, in terms of x

$y = $ _____

(a) Hence find
y when $x = 1.6$

Answer $y = $ _____

x when $y = 125$

Answer $x = $ _____

63 (a) (i) Factorise $3a^2 + 6a$

Answer _____

(ii) Hence simplify
(Hint: 'Hence' means you should use your previous answer)

$$\frac{3a^2 + 6a}{a^2 - 4}$$

Answer _____

(b) (i) Factorise $x^2 - 2x - 3$

Answer _____

(ii) Hence simplify
$$\frac{x^2 - 2x - 3}{x^2 - 5x + 6}$$

Answer _____

(c) (i) Factorise $t^2 + 11t + 28$

Answer _____

(ii) Hence simplify
$$\frac{t^2 + 11t + 28}{t^2 + 5t - 14}$$

Answer _____

64 The rectangle and square below both have the same area.

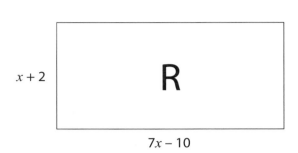

$x + 2$ · R · $7x - 10$

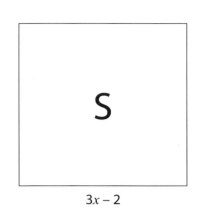

S · $3x - 2$

(a) Prove that $x^2 - 8x + 12 = 0$

(b) Hence find 2 possible values for x.

Answer $x =$ _____

65 The straight line $y = x + 3$ cuts the curve $x^2 + y^2 = 29$ at two points.
   (a) Prove that $x^2 + 3x - 10 = 0$

(b) Hence find the coordinates of the points.

Answer (_____,_____) ,(_____,_____)

A* Questions

1 Find the exact value of the following:

(a) $4^{\frac{1}{2}}$

Answer _____

(b) $27^{-\frac{1}{3}}$

Answer _____

(c) $32^{-\frac{3}{5}}$

Answer _____

(d) $16^{-0.25}$

Answer _____

(e) $100^{-1.5}$

Answer _____

2 Solve the following:

(a) $\dfrac{9}{x-3} + \dfrac{4}{x-4} = 5$

Answer $x =$ _____

(b) $\dfrac{10}{x+1} - \dfrac{2}{x-2} = 1$

Answer $x =$ _____

(c) $\dfrac{4}{1-x} - \dfrac{8}{x-1} = 3$

Answer $x =$ _____

3 Solve $y - 2x + 11 = 0$ and $y^2 = x^2 - 7$

Answer $x =$ _____

$y =$ _____

4 Find the coordinates of the two points where the straight line $2x - y = 10$ cuts the curve $x^2 - 8x + y^2 = 9$

Answer _____

5 Simplify the following
(**Hint: Factorise the numerator and the denominator. Do not try to simplify your answer further than it will simplify**)

(a) $\dfrac{x^2 - 2x - 15}{x^2 - 9}$

Answer _____

(b) $\dfrac{x^2 - 10x + 21}{x^2 - x - 6}$

Answer _____

(c) $\dfrac{2x^2 + x - 6}{6x^2 - 11x + 3}$

Answer _____

(d) $\dfrac{16x^2 - 1}{12x^2 + 3x}$

Answer _____

(e) $\dfrac{x^2 - x - 2}{x^2 - 7x + 10}$

Answer _____

(f) $\dfrac{x^2 + 7x + 12}{x^2 + 2x - 8}$

Answer _____

6 A ship sails 7.8 km on a bearing of 041° from a harbour H until it reaches port P. It then sails 8.4 km on a bearing of 126° from P until it reaches port Q.
Calculate
(a) the distance HQ
   (Hint: Make a sketch)

Answer _____ km

(b) the bearing of H from Q

Answer _____ °

7 There are 456 men, 342 women and 513 children on a holiday package.
The tour operator wants to take a stratified sample of men, women and children of size 69.
How many men will be included in this sample?

Answer _____ men

8 The histogram below shows the heights in cm of different objects.

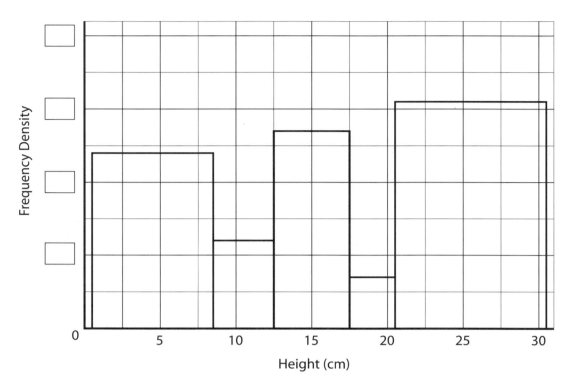

768 objects have heights between 1 and 8 cm, measured to the nearest cm.

(a) Write down the scale of the vertical axis.

Answer 1 cm = _____

(b) Complete the vertical axis.

(c) Hence complete the table below.

Height (cm)	Frequency
1 - 8	768

Answers

1 (b) 2 cm

2 (a) $y = 2x - 10$ **(b)** $y = 2x + 9$

3 (a) 86, 164, 204, 232 **(b)** points plotted, curve **(c), (d)** & **(e)** Check answers from pupil's graph

4 (a) $3n + 4$ **(b)** $26 - 2n$ **(c)** $7n - 5$

5 (a) $(4x - 3)(2n + c)$ **(b)** $(q - 8)(q + 5)$ **(c)** $(f + 3)(-4f - 5)$ **(d)** $3(t - 4v)(t + 4v)$

6 (a) $0, -\frac{1}{6}$ **(b)** $3, 6$

7 $AB^2 = 37$ $BC^2 = 37$ $AC^2 = 74$ $\therefore$ $AC^2 = AB^2 + BC^2$ Proof by Pythagoras
or grad AB = 6, grad BC = $\frac{-1}{6}$, product = -1 so $\angle$ ABC is 90°

8 (a) $9\frac{4}{9}$ **(b)** $\frac{9}{10}$ **(c)** $12\frac{4}{15}$

9 $x = -2$ $y = 6$

10 (a) 34° **(b)** 34° **(c)** 112° **(d)** 68°

11 216, 18, 344, 43

12 (a) $\frac{11}{5}$ **(b)** 8 **(c)** 5

13 (a) $\frac{(m^2 - n^2)}{nm}$ **(b)** $\frac{n^2 + 24}{nm}$ **(c)** $\frac{11q}{4}$

14 (a) $p = 3$ **(b)** $q = -6$

15 50.2°

16 Q1 No answer box for 0 homeworks, Q2 No answer box for T = 120 mins

17 (b) 2 cm

18 (a) $y = -4x + 2$ **(b)** $y = -4x + 8$ **(c)** $y = \frac{1}{4}x - 4$

19 (a) $-5, -2$ **(b)** $\frac{7}{4}, \frac{-7}{4}$ **(c)** $5, -8$

20 (a) 56° **(b)** 62° **(c)** 28° **(d)** 152° (cyclic quadrilateral property)

21 (a) $\frac{5}{2}, -\frac{5}{2}$ **(b)** $7, -5$ **(c)** $-\frac{4}{3}, 2$ **(d)** $-\frac{5}{2}, -\frac{2}{3}$ **(e)** $2, 4$

22 (b) (i) some classes are smaller than others **(ii)** not everyone is a homeowner

24 Frequency density: 38, 27, 34, 22, 14, 26

25 Draw quadrilateral inside circle. Join the centre to two opposite vertices. Use the angle at the centre equal to twice the angle at the circumference.

26 (a) $8x^2 - 22xy - 21y^2$ **(b)** $25a^2 - 60ab + 36b^2$ **(c)** $-k^2 - 2\,km - 17m^2$

27 (a) $y = -\frac{4}{3}x + 8$ **(b)** $\frac{3}{4}$

28 (b) (0 , −4) and (5 , 11)

29 (a) $x = -6$

30 (a) 6 or $\frac{3}{2}$ **(b)** 2 or $-\frac{4}{3}$

31 (a) Alternate segment theorem **(b)** Opposite angles in a cyclic quadrilateral add up to 180° **(c)** Angle between a tangent and a radius is 90° **(d)** 104°

32 (a) 331 **(b)** bar between 110 and 140 cm with frequency density 3.4

33 (a) $y = 4x + 2$ **(a)** $y = -\frac{1}{2}x + 2\frac{1}{2}$

34 (a) 1.01 **(b)** 12.2 **(c)** 0.467 **(d)** 721

35 (a) 9 times bigger **(a)** 4 times smaller

36 (2, 4) $(\frac{-4}{5}, \frac{-22}{5})$

37 $x = 3$ or $\frac{4}{5}$

38 (a) $p = -\frac{3}{2}q$ **(b)** $-\frac{1}{4}$

39 (a) 66.4° **(b)** 5.74 cm

40 Least = 102.55 cm, Greatest = 103.25 cm

41(a) 4% **(b)** £5600 **(c)** £6299.24

42 (a) 7.2 cm **(b)** 11.8 cm

43 (a) 0.67 m **(b)** 51°

44 4 years

45 (a) 208.05 cm **(b)** 77.64 cm

46 18.3 cm²

47 (a) 15 m **(b)** 28.3 m

48 (i) 494.375 cm³ **(ii)** 4.44 cm

49 (a) 3 4 5 6 **(c) (i)** 0.6 **(ii)** 7

50 3.77 cm

51 (a) 2.54, –0.788 **(b)** 0.198, –4.20

52 (a) 9.36 cm **(b)** 5.32 cm **(c)** 62.9° **(d)** 57°

53 (b) 6, $\frac{9}{8}$

54 13.6 cm²

55 21.4 cm²

56 (a) 11.5 cm **(b)** 20.4° **(c)** 22.9°

57 (a) 27.5625 **(b)** 1.08 **(c)** 2.5

58 (a) 67° **(b)** 9.33 cm **(c)** 3.84 cm or 3.85 cm

59 77.1°

60 $a = 8$ $b = -3$

61 (a) 58° **(b)** 116° **(c)** 32° **(d)** 64°

62 (a) $y = -\dfrac{20}{x^2}$ **(b)(i)** 7.8125 **(ii)** 0.4

63 (a)(i) $3a(a + 2)$ **(ii)** $\dfrac{3a}{a - 2}$ **(b)(i)** $(x - 3)(x + 1)$ **(ii)** $\dfrac{x + 1}{x - 2}$ **(c)(i)** $(t + 4)(t + 7)$ **(ii)** $\dfrac{t + 4}{t - 2}$

64 (b) 2, 6

65 (b) (2, 5) (–5, –2)

A* Questions

1 (a) $\frac{1}{2}$ **(b)** $\frac{1}{3}$ **(c)** $\frac{1}{8}$ **(d)** $\frac{1}{2}$ **(e)** $\frac{1}{1000}$

2 (a) 6 or $\frac{18}{5}$ **(b)** 4 or 5 **(c)** –3

3 $x = 4, y = -3$ and $x = \frac{32}{3}, y = \frac{31}{3}$

4 (7, 4) and $(\frac{13}{5}, -\frac{24}{5})$

5 (a) $\dfrac{x - 5}{x - 3}$ **(b)** $\dfrac{x - 7}{x + 2}$ **(c)** $\dfrac{x + 2}{3x - 1}$ **(d)** $\dfrac{4x - 1}{3x}$ **(e)** $\dfrac{x + 1}{x - 5}$ **(f)** $\dfrac{x + 3}{x - 2}$

6 (a) 11.95 km or 12.0 km **(b)** 265°

7 24

8 (a) 20

   (b) 40, 80, 120, 160

   (c)

9–12	13–17	18–20	21–30
192	640	84	1240